One-to-One

Managing quality time with individuals for engagement and success

5WH

Robertson Hunter Stewart

This book is dedicated to:

Adrian Ellis

"An attentive mentor and friend"

The author of this work is:

Robertson Hunter Stewart
Born 1962, St Andrews, Scotland

Other books from the same author:

The Incredible Value of **Employee Power** Unleashed, How to gain competitive advantage by treating your employees well!

ISBN: 9781076872159 – June 2019 available on:

Amazon:

US: https://www.amazon.com/dp/1076872158

FR: https://www.amazon.fr/dp/1076872158

Also available on: Apple and Kobo (Fnac)

www.robertsonhunterstewart.com

Follow the author on:
Robertson Hunter Stewart @:

FOREWORD

Employee engagement, together with its importance and contribution to the overall success of business, is one of the most talked about and strategic subjects today across all companies, organisations and sectors. In particular, how do you set about trying to improve on your employees' level of engagement with their work, the organisation and, most of all, with their managers? Before looking at some of the statistics regarding this subject, let's look first at how we might define employee engagement?

According to me, engaged employees are:

"Those who find true purpose in the workplace and who are committed to their work and those they work with."

It is therefore extremely disconcerting to discover that according to recent studies on the subject of employee engagement only about one in ten employees are **actually engaged in the workplace**! This is not good news, of course, as the lack of engagement engenders higher than necessary costs to all organisations. Consider, for example, that similar recent studies go on to show that companies with **higher engagement** have a **productivity** level, which is significantly higher and are over 20% **more profitable** than other companies.

If we now look at a couple of the underlying reasons for these results, we probably won't be very surprised. First and foremost, low employee engagement does, of course, lead to higher turnover and, when we know that the average cost of recruiting, selecting and onboarding a new entry-level employee is approximately **$5000** today, we would do well to retain our talent. This is without even considering the less easy to calculate cost of losing experienced and talented employees. Other recent polls have shown that highly **engaged workplaces** also report around **40% less absenteeism.**

It is very easy to see then that a lack of engagement from your employees will definitely cost your company money and lower than expected profits. This is already bad enough for any business, but it's far from all. The financial losses might already be more or less short term depending on whether or not corrective action has or will be taken by your company. In the long term, however, the negative effects on innovation and the competitive positioning of your company are likely to be nothing short of disastrous. In other words, the very sustainability of your organisation may well be put in question if no action is taken to improve engagement. As mentioned, people will leave and when they do they take their experience, their "good will" and their ideas with them. Quite apart from the immediate short-term financial aspects and impacts on recruitment, your company may find it difficult to recruit due to a less than optimal employer reputation. Obviously, if this becomes a serious problem you can very quickly get to a situation where your company is no longer in a position to operate correctly.

All of this is telling us two things: employee engagement matters and it matters an awful lot! So the most pertinent question to ask ourselves is very probably what we should be doing today about **employee engagement** so as **to ensure** that our company continues to **remain both viable and competitive?**

Based on other recent research, it would seem that a big part of the answer to this question is to do with the appreciation and recognition of employees; this appears to be fundamental. Certain recent studies show that **69% of employees say that they would work harder if they were better appreciated.** According to other recent polls, when employees were asked what would be the most important thing a manager could do to help an employee succeed, the most common response by far (at nearly 40%) was that **recognition was the most important form of support**.

Having scanned the majority of the information and statistics currently available on this subject (as of June 2020), **recognition and appreciation** are the two factors which appear to have the most impact on improving employee engagement. This probably comes as little surprise to most of us; however, the next piece of information certainly might.

According to several recent surveys on rewarding and recognition, nearly **50% of the people surveyed prefer to receive recognition from their manager on a private one-to-one basis,** with only around 10% wishing for this to happen in public. Further research from several well-known academic institutes support claims that face to face meetings are by far the most valuable form of communication.

All of this then leads us to the very obvious conclusion that the way forward has an awful lot to do with the way we interact with our individual team members in the workplace.

This also explains to a large extent why this book puts managing and communicating with individuals at the very heart of continuing, sustainable success for all companies. It will show you how to best use your most important commodity – **time** – in the service of your most important resource – your **employees.** Last, but by no means least, knowing how to interact with and manage your people better than your competitors will become a fundamental source of competitive advantage.

As managers, we all spend a tremendous amount of our time in meetings with all of the various stakeholders in our organisations. After all, the very essence of our role as managers is about communicating effectively with others. As managers, we should in fact be spending the majority of our time talking to people within the organisation.

What we spend a lot less time doing is preparing a **communications strategy** for talking to others, as might be the case in other parts of our business such as sales and finance, for example. This book is about just that – the very essence of our role as managers, in other words, how to talk to people and gain sustainable competitive advantage by fully **engaging** our employees with both ourselves and the company or organisation.

This book will demonstrate the importance of treating your collaborators, not just as team members but also as **individuals**. It will give a very precise framework as to how to improve communication with individual team members, through the use of a structured framework. It will also show the importance of building those oh so important working relationships based on **confidence**

and trust and it will outline exactly how to go about this.

The book will give precise detail(s) about just why it's so important to give quality time to your employees and just how to go about this in the most strategic and structured way possible. If you already have one-to-one meetings in place with your managers and staff, it will tell you how to improve on this in order to increase engagement from and to give purpose to the individuals that make up those teams.

If not yet in place, the book will give you step-by-step guidance on how to put one-to-one meetings in place successfully, whilst showing exactly why these meetings are an extremely important part of the foundation needed to successfully manage your teams and organisation, **and how they will ultimately lead to improved engagement in your place of work.**

TABLE OF CONTENTS

INTRODUCTION

One-to-One

Managing quality time with individuals for engagement and success

5WH

INTRODUCTION

Let me start with a question: have you ever had the experience where you desperately needed to see your boss but he or she was just not available? Going further than that, perhaps it's already happened on several previous occasions to the point where you start to think: "Yep, they definitely just don't want to see me." If this happens all of the time or on a consistent basis, you are going to end up thinking that the boss doesn't care at all and, at some point, you are going to stop caring or go and find a job somewhere else where the boss does seem to care about you as an individual.

Either that or you will end up staying in the job, but you will not be at all motivated by what you are doing and, in the end, not caring. Not a healthy situation for yourself, your hierarchy or the organisation.

Well, quite probably, it's not that the boss doesn't want to see you (we hope!) but that he just can't seem to find the time to fit you into his agenda!

One of the biggest problems that managers and supervisors at all levels have today is the limited time they have available to accomplish everything they have to do. This can be stressful and often we find ourselves asking the question: "Are we making the best use of our time?" However, this is not the only question that we should be asking ourselves as managers in this regard. Should we not also be querying whether or not we are optimising our team members' time?

As managers, one of the first things that we should all be doing is trying to gauge the value of the time that we are spending on whatever the task at hand might be. We have all heard the expression "time is money." Well, it certainly is in the workplace where all aspects of return on investment are crucial. If we look at most general management models, there are three main areas where anyone in a management position should be spending some of their time: the task, the team and the individual.

All things being equal then, and if everything were completely rational in the classical sense (in a world of perfect information where our cognitive capacities are always at 100% and we know 100% of our own preferences), we might be tempted to think: "Yeah, ok, I'll spend a third of my time on the tasks, a third with the team and a third with individuals from my teams." This might work, to some extent, but it would be very hard to keep track of and might very well prove ineffective as well as somewhat counterproductive. Nevertheless, I would suggest that you spend **at least** one third of your time as a manager on managing individuals from and within your teams.

That's not to say that you should be micro-managing every single person in your team. This would very quickly become extremely unhealthy and lead to a situation where the team members perceive it as a lack of trust and confidence in their competence, and/or their ability to do their jobs. What I am saying is that the time spent with the individuals in the team should be time **well spent** – in other words, it should be **quality time**.

So just what is this notion of quality time? My definition of quality time spent with individual team members would be as follows:

Time where both of the participants get something valuable from the conversation and which adds value to the organisation.

This definition highlights the fact that having quality one-to-one meetings is profitable for you, the employee and the organisation. For you and the employee, it's an opportunity to build a working relationship based on mutual understanding and trust. For the organisation as a whole, it can and does lead to a position of sustainable competitive advantage and enhanced profits.

This is what this book is all about, optimising the value of the time that you spend with the individuals on your team and making sure that you do enough of this. If we go back to the concept of return on investment, both you and your employee are investing time in this so you must make sure that you both gain from it as much as possible in **as many ways as possible**.

The framework that I have used for this book is the use of pertinent questions, namely 5WH questions, as follows:

> ➢ What
> ➢ Why
> ➢ When
> ➢ Where
> ➢ Who

This is followed by a section with detailed guidelines for one-to-one meetings focusing on:

> ➢ How (explaining exactly how to run a one-to-meeting in the most effective way possible)

I have used this framework in order to facilitate learning and to give an easy to follow and practical guide to the one-to-one meeting process. I have also used this method because these are the questions that we as managers often use in our day-to-day decision-making process in all areas of our business.

The main purpose of the book is to help managers and supervisors optimise and add additional value to time spent with their team members on an individual basis. Said another way, it's about **spending the right amount of time with team members in the right way.**

In the end, it's very simple; if you want your employees to engage with you as a manager, you have no choice but to spend quality time with them.

Let's now start by looking at just what a one-to-one meeting should look like.

WHAT

One-to-One

Managing quality time with individuals for engagement and success

5WH

WHAT

So what exactly is a one-to-one meeting?

Well, first and foremost, it is a meeting where you will be spending time with an individual team member as opposed to the team as a whole. Secondly, and perhaps more importantly, it is neither an informal meeting, nor just a quick chat! Too often, as managers, we spend far too much of our time meeting with employees and talking to them in an informal way (for example at the coffee machine). This is not necessarily a bad thing in itself as long as it doesn't take up too much of your or your employee's time. A one-to-one is a meeting where you are going to discuss a number of different subjects with your employee in a **formal** and **structured** way. This is also a meeting in which you should be meeting with your direct reports (N-1) only.

It is not a meeting where the employee is called to the office for a quick chat not knowing why they have been called in the first place and, even worse, leaving the office five minutes later being none the wiser (you know what I'm talking about here, right?). The team member should have an extremely clear idea of what the meeting is going to be about and exactly what his/her role or contribution is to be in this meeting.

Some employees (at whatever level, managers included) might not be used to this kind of approach at all and need to be reassured as to the purpose of the meeting and what exactly is expected from them during the meeting (their role): "Am I to sit there and listen while the boss blabbers on for god knows how long? Am I expected to speak about something at some point and, if so, about what exactly?"

To avoid these types of unnecessary (and often stress-inducing) questions, it should be explained to the employee that this is to be a **highly participative meeting** and, even more than that, it should be explained to them that they have "ownership" of this meeting. One of the best ways to get the point across here is to use the very first one-to-one meeting to explain to the team member in detail what is expected from them in future meetings, how often these meetings are to take place and that this is "his (or her) time." Other important information to give to the employee during this explanation is just why the meeting is named as either a one-to-one meeting or quality time, and you should underline just how significant this is.

To ensure the success and additional value of these meetings, we as managers must ensure in every way possible that the employee not only understands the purpose of these meetings but that they are comfortable with the entire concept and the process. This is particularly important if these types of meetings have not been held before within the organisation. You do need to explain why these meetings are so important to them and also why they are important to you as a manager and to the organisation as a whole. For example, there is nothing wrong with saying to an employee: "One of the reasons for these meetings is that I really need to hear more of your ideas on how we can improve the shop floor operations" or "We need to spend more time together to look over and track the yearly objectives that we have set together for this year."

My suggestion is that these meetings should last for a minimum of one hour in order to give adequate time for some in-depth communication and relationship building. And don't worry if the time goes a little bit over as this will always be time well spent. Earlier, we said that these meetings should be formalised and structured. An important part of this is the fact that there should be written minutes of these meetings. This is to ensure that the next time you meet; you know what was said, what was agreed and what the topics for future discussion are. In summary, it helps ensure that meetings are coherent and avoids covering "old ground." In addition, this will also go a long way to ensuring commitment on agreements and decisions made during the meetings.

From a management perspective, it is crucial to ensure that the correct level of importance is given to and seen to be given to these meetings by management at all levels. It is vital that when the meetings have been scheduled they should not be cancelled except under exceptional circumstances (there's a fire in the building!). Furthermore, do remember that a one-to-one is an excellent opportunity to listen to your direct reports and that important and sometimes information critical to the overall good running of the organisation will be shared.

So, in summary, a one-to-one meeting should:

- Be as participative as possible
- Have a clear purpose
- Have adequate time for in-depth discussion
- Be clearly defined (what are you going to talk about?)
- Be frequent
- Be formal (with minutes taken at each meeting)
- Be a source of commitment to action

That's enough about what a one-to-one meeting is. What about what you are going to discuss? To that end, I have always found it useful to discuss the following topics:

- How the person is getting along in general (how are they?)

- ➢ How are they getting on with the other team members (particularly important when the person is new to the organisation)
- ➢ How things are going on the shop floor
- ➢ Discussion about areas for improvement in operations
- ➢ A point on his or her objectives
- ➢ Resources (does the team member have adequate tools to do their job?)

This list of bullet points gives some very good pointers to areas for discussion but is by no means exhaustive. What is actually discussed in these meetings will be determined to a large extent, of course, by the evolving operational and strategic priorities of the organisation. Establishing priorities for discussion will be important and a great tool for doing this will be discussed in a later chapter.

Never forget that these meetings are privileged moments for your team members where they should always have your **undivided attention**. They are also a fantastic opportunity to build the employee's engagement with both you and the organisation, but especially with you, their manager. Don't forget people work for people not for companies. Let's now go on to look at just why exactly all of this is so tremendously important.

WHY

One-to-One

Managing quality time with individuals for engagement and success

5WH

WHY

As to why we should carry out one-to-one meetings, this is **the fundamental question**. What really is the purpose of taking the time to meet with your direct reports formally and regularly on a one-to-one basis?

To start answering this question, let us imagine exactly the contrary, that you never meet with your direct reports in any fashion whatsoever, in whatever kind of way, either formal or informal! I'm sure that we would all agree that under these circumstances, it would be extremely difficult or nigh on impossible to manage your people. I think that as managers, we would all agree that it is impossible to manage people in a situation where there is a lack of communication or worse none at all.

Not only that, but you risk the total disengagement of your team members, which will in turn lead to a lack of motivation, and, in the end, you will probably find that turnover will be on the increase whilst productivity decreases. Thus, you will incur unnecessary recruitment and training costs and this of course is not the way that you want to run a business.

So, let's say for the sake of argument that we do meet with them, but only within the context of team meetings where the whole team is present. Well, this is already better than the first scenario as you might actually see all of the team members, but will you hear all of them or each of them? The answer is most probably not. Not everyone is predisposed to talk or announce their ideas or concerns in front of others. Remember that people are all ultimately unique individuals; every single one of us is different. Even the more extrovert members of the team might find it strange if you never make time to see them on an individual basis.

The mere fact that you take the time to meet with individuals one-to-one is already in itself a form of recognition. What you are saying to them is: "Yes, you are important enough that I make time for you." Recognition is important to just about everyone; we all like to know how we are doing, how we are seen by those that we work with and to get "a pat on the back" from time to time. If we have the feeling that "we are just a number" we are not likely to find purpose or motivation in what we do. Giving time to people is, then, one of the keys to motivation and engagement.

According to several reliable sources, more than two thirds of the variance in employee engagement scores can be accounted for by the relationship that a manager has with their direct reports.

Furthermore, these studies go on to say that 50% of employees have quit a job at one time or another during their career as a direct consequence of their boss or the boss's behaviour. I would further suggest that the managers in question here do not give adequate or the right kind of time to the employees. In not doing so, they help create the conditions in which toxic work cultures can flourish, such as a blame culture.

As managers, we all know that people who are both motivated and engaged with the organisation are far more likely to be highly productive and loyal. Although being well paid is important for people at work, employees will only go that extra mile if they are listened to, motivated and recognised for what they are doing. **People need to have a purpose at work** and listening attentively to them during a one-to-one is a very good way of reinforcing a healthy working relationship with your employee.

If we now go back to what we said earlier about all of us being unique individuals: we all have aspirations, hopes, dreams and fears, some of which may be shared and some not. Every single one of us is unique and needs to be treated as a unique individual. Nevertheless, in the workplace, there are some areas that offer common ground to all individuals and one of the most important is to be given **purpose** at work.

One of the main underlying principles of carrying out one-to-one meetings is to give purpose to your employee's time so that they engage with both yourself as the manager and the organisation. Following on from this, one of the most important things to do during a one-to-one is to be **specific about purpose** through the creation and putting in place of objectives. The objectives should be agreed with the employee and should be extremely clear and precise.

Let's further underline all of this by talking about personal objectives which should, of course, in the interest of clarity, always be SMART:

- ➢ **Specific and simple**
- ➢ **Measurable**
- ➢ **Achievable and agreed**
- ➢ **Relevant**
- ➢ **Timed**

Please note two things regarding SMART, as defined above. For the S, you can see that objectives should not only be specific but also simple. Simple here does not mean easy; it means that the objective should be clear and precise and understandable. Simply said (no pun intended), an objective can be as specific as we like, but if it's not fully understood or if, as a manager, we have not checked for understanding on the part of the employee, we will not obtain the hoped-for result(s).

Furthermore, concerning the achievable aspect of the objective, a second A for agreed has been added. This is because, far too often, we have a tendency to assume that the employee in front of us agrees with the objective when sometimes this is just not the case at all. He or she might, for example, think that the objective is not at all achievable! If he or she thinks that and says nothing in this regard, there is a good chance that they will not achieve it. Gaining agreement on the objective is therefore important, in order to ensure the correct level of motivation. In other words, to ensure that the person is ok with doing it and actually **believes** that they can achieve it!

So, let's now imagine that you have sat down with your direct report and, using the SMART method, you have agreed on the objectives for the entire year. You could say that this is an excellent starting point and you would be right. Let's further imagine that during the course of the year external factors which are completely beyond both your employee's and your own control make it nigh on impossible to achieve a certain number of objectives set at the beginning of the year. Are you the type of manager who is going to leave these objectives in place and expect results from your subordinate in any case? Are you going to wait until the end of the year in question only to discover, aghast, that none of the objectives have been achieved?

Let's say that you do just that and wait till the end of the year at the next annual evaluation (appraisal interview), where you discover that the employee has not reached the objectives set at the beginning of the year. Perhaps the non-completion of the objectives is due to external factors and perhaps not. For example, the employee might have needed further resources, advice, help or coaching from you to better achieve what he or she was asked to do but never had the opportunity to speak to you about it!

Of course, at this stage, you could always just ask or tell the employee: "You should have come and seen me before; this is your fault! Why did you not come and ask for help before it was too late?" I think that you might agree though that this would not be the best approach, or indeed even fair. As a manager, if blame is to be apportioned here you should be blaming yourself. That is to say, if you had been meeting with your employee on a regular basis during the course of the year, you would have had opportunities to look at how he or she was getting on with the objectives in question. During these meetings, you would have had the opportunity to discuss external factors that might be affecting an objective and perhaps modify the objective in light of this information (for example, an economic downturn which makes it impossible for the employee to attain his or her production objectives).

Throughout these meetings, he or she would also have had the opportunity to ask for extra help or resources and explain to you why without these resources it might be impossible to attain the objective which was originally set.

It's easy to see that holding these one-to-one meetings during the course of the year would have avoided a situation where there is a big surprise at the end of the year when you discover that not much has been achieved. In the very worst scenario and if you have a culture of "blame" at work, the appraisal interview at the end of the year is going to resemble more of a disciplinary interview than an annual performance review! This is quite obviously neither fair nor productive for anyone concerned.

It seems extremely clear that having regular one-to-one meetings in place will avoid the type of situation just described and help to keep objectives in line with requirements whilst taking into account both internal and external changes during the course of the year. It also lets both you and the employee take remedial action when and where necessary by adapting to changes as required.

Another reason that these meetings are so important is to do with the sharing of information. We all know the expression "information is power" and this is so true in any organisation as, without information that is clear, accurate, precise and timely, it can become extremely difficult to run any company or organisation, in particular, organisations which have an extremely vertical structure of their hierarchy (top-down). This is still the case in most organisations, whatever articles on this subject might be saying, i.e., there's still a boss somewhere.

Let's put all of this another way:

1. If you don't meet with your subordinates at all, you will have no information and, in the absence of information, you will not be in a position to make decisions (or good decisions in any case).

2. If you don't meet with your subordinates on a regular basis, the information that you have will not be timely (recent enough); once again, decisions based on this information will quite probably not prove to be optimal.

3. If you do meet with your subordinates on a regular basis, but the objective or purpose of the meeting is not clear, you may obtain information, but it runs the risk of not being very clear or precise. In addition to this, the employee will not "buy into" the one-to-one process so there will be a lack of trust or confidence. Under these circumstances, the quality of information obtained is likely to be quite poor.

If we put together 1 to 3 from above, it's fairly easy to see that if you do want to "keep your finger on the pulse" you need to be holding these meetings in a way that ensures they are frequent and well-structured and that the employee in question really has **"bought into the process."**

In addition, the fact that you are having regular meetings which are structured and where the employee is given the opportunity to express themselves will eventually lead to the building of confidence and trust and, in the vast majority of cases, this will lead to an increase in the volume and quality of information shared.

But it's not just about information that you might receive, these meetings are also a great way to pass on information or important messages to your employees. Although you should not be doing most of the talking in these meetings, you should definitely be doing some talking: giving advice, answering questions or passing on important information. At the same time, the way that you communicate and encourage the employee to participate will allow you once again the opportunity to strengthen your relationship based on mutual trust and confidence. There's a great quote that underlines the importance of strengthening relationships with your reports:

"People don't care how much you know until they know how much you care."

Theodore Roosevelt

From my own experience and from conversations with many managers and leaders over the years, this phrase has proven over and over again how important trust is with reference to effective communication.

As a bonus, during regular meetings like this, it is likely that at some moments the employee may decide to expose an idea that they have had and if the idea in question turns out to be a massive "game changer" for the organisation then you will certainly have the return on the time invested that we spoke about earlier. Care must be taken though, as not all ideas will be good or even possible to put into practice. Nevertheless, it is important to give feedback regarding the ideas, whether this is immediately or in a subsequent meeting, so as to actively encourage this type of sharing with your subordinates. A lot of the time you should, though, give feedback on their ideas at the next meeting. This gives you more time to think about it and, at the same time, you don't give the impression that you "shoved an idea away" without some careful consideration.

In addition, if the idea put forward proves to be excellent, relevant and possible to put in place, the transition from idea to action is likely to be frictionless! This is, of course, due to the fact that it will already have the full support of your team member. This is as opposed to ideas which are imposed or are the product of a more top-down style where, as you know, you are likely to see a lot more resistance.

Last, but by no means least, as a manager and as mentioned in the introduction, you have to try to ensure that you manage your time correctly or in as optimal a fashion as possible. We have all heard the expression "plan your work and then work your plan" and you're most probably also aware of the five Ps of planning:

> ➤ Proper
> ➤ Planning
> ➤ Prevents
> ➤ Poor
> ➤ Performance

As a manager or supervisor, at any level, you are probably interrupted quite often or perhaps even very often by team members or subordinates wanting to ask you questions or in need of information that only you can provide. If you don't schedule time for this through meetings, it is more than likely going to become a problem in the sense that the frequency of these interruptions might become far too high and you will no longer be planning anything! Under these circumstances, you will not be in control of your time or "working your plan"; you will only be reacting to circumstances and situations instead of being proactive. In planning one-to-one meetings, you are in fact reducing the need for your employees to "interrupt" you as you will have provided the necessary time for them through the one-to-one meetings.

What we are really saying here is that, although holding these meetings does take time, it will save you a lot of time in the long run.

So, in summary, as to why we should hold one-to-one meetings, they allow us to:

- ➤ Recognise the importance of individuals
- ➤ Monitor performance during the course of the year
- ➤ Adjust objectives when, and if necessary
- ➤ Build relationships with our employees based on confidence and trust
- ➤ Heighten the engagement, motivation and productivity of our employees
- ➤ Reduce unnecessary recruitment and training costs related to high turnover
- ➤ Ensure better decision making for management, based on timely and accurate information from the "shop floor"
- ➤ Create the opportunity to pick up on great ideas from employees
- ➤ Find out how team members feel
- ➤ Better manage our time

In conclusion, it's what we call in the "jargon" a "no brainer" to ensure that you have regular quality time with individual team members.

Let's now go and have a look at when we should be holding these one-to-one meetings.

WHEN

One-to-One

Managing quality time with individuals for engagement and success

5WH

WHEN

At first view, this might not seem particularly important and you might be tempted to say, based on what we have seen: "Well, as long as it's fairly regular it shouldn't matter should it?"

What if we start by asking ourselves the question about how often we should be holding these meetings? Is there a minimum or maximum frequency? In my experience, the absolute minimum frequency would be at the end of each quarter (or once every three months). However, do remember what we said earlier about timely information which helps towards making well-informed decisions. Strictly speaking, at whatever level an employee is currently at, this will at least give opportunities to gauge performance compared to quarterly results.

I have in the past been in the habit of holding these meetings with senior managers in my executive teams on a monthly basis. This gave each of them time to prepare between meetings and also avoided interfering with their operational responsibilities. To go further, I would suggest that this is an extremely good cycle for employees at any level whether or not they are in a supervisory/managerial position. There is one exception here though and it's quite a big one. For line staff, we might actually consider having these one-to-one meetings more often but for less time; in some cases it might be a good idea to have meetings with your line staff once a week!

And now I hear you say but that's far too much: "If we do that, they will never be on the shop floor!" Consider this, however; if we organise this time correctly and ensure that it is correctly structured, perhaps we can avoid unnecessary interruptions in production (for a secondary industry) or unnecessary questions about how to deal with a client (in the tertiary sector) as a problem with production may be pointed out during a one-to-one or, in the second case, the way to treat the client may have already been discussed.

This also makes sense from the point of view of delegation and empowerment. Normally, employees should have more and more autonomy and be more empowered as they take on added responsibility. Therefore, they should definitely have less need for frequent interaction with their direct superior as this autonomy grows (in other words, as they take on more of a supervisory or managerial role).

Having said all of that, one-to-one meetings on a monthly basis would seem to be a reasonable frequency for most employees across any organisation.

So, what about the best time of day to have a one-to-one meeting?

Well, for one thing, do avoid holding these meetings just after lunch! As we all know from a physiological point of view, whilst our body is digesting food this does lower blood sugar levels and leads to tiredness and in a lot of cases sleepiness. I think most of us have experienced these "symptoms" ourselves at one time or another and it's probably easy to see that we won't have the optimum conditions here in terms of alertness, awareness or productivity.

With more senior managers I have often been in the habit of planning these meetings just before lunch and then having lunch with the person just after. This is a great way to do things as it gives an opportunity to do all of the formal follow up and discussion first, followed by a more informal type of discussion during lunch.

Another key moment to avoid when planning a one-to-one meeting is when activity on the "shop floor" is at its peak. Let's have a look at some examples of moments to avoid from different sectors of activity:

- ➢ Saturday afternoon in a shop or supermarket
- ➢ Lunchtime in a restaurant
- ➢ Eleven in the morning at the reception of a hotel (when all the clients are checking out)
- ➢ On a Saturday night at a police station or a hospital

Although we could have looked at many more examples, the point here is to avoid pulling people away from their jobs during peak activity times. This avoids two things:

1. Adversely affecting the efficiency and effectiveness of operations during the peak activity time itself.
2. The situation where the employee whom you are speaking to is "not there" when you are supposed to be having this important discussion because he or she is still thinking or worrying about what's happening in the operation.

What about optimal times during the day for meetings, what might those be? Well, as we've already said, not directly after lunchtime. What about first thing in the morning then? Well, it might be better than just after lunch, but having a meeting first thing in the morning with an employee means they might still be sleepy and that they've not had time to prepare properly. What about near the end of the working day then, would this be optimal? It might not be, due to the fact that the employee could be thinking that it's time to go home soon, rather than concentrating on the content of the meeting.

Taking all of this into account (if we are talking about a nine to five day), it leaves us with two possible time slots which might be more optimal: either mid-morning, just before lunch, as already discussed, or in the afternoon around three o'clock when energy levels are likely to be higher than directly after lunch.

This might be seen as an excess of planning by some, but, if we believe as we should that these quality-time meetings are the very cornerstone of our people strategy, everything has to be done to ensure that they are as effective as possible.

In that case then, what about optimal days during the week?

Well, let's pretend that we are talking about a working week, which goes from Monday to Friday. What about Monday then? Might that be an optimal day for a meeting? Well, maybe not as people have just got back to work after the weekend and take a little time to readjust to the working environment. On top of that they might be a little tired, so concentration will probably not be optimal.

As for Friday, the employee might already be planning their weekend and "watching the clock" so to speak. So, once again, we might find ourselves in a meeting with an employee who has other things on their mind, so probably not the best time to be planning a meeting either.

The good news is that you still have three days left! On the midweek days, the employee is more likely to be in a "work rhythm", have better energy levels, and be more available and predisposed to having such a meeting. Remember that it's not only you as the manager who has to concentrate during these meetings but also the employee, so everything that you can do to create optimal conditions for this meeting should and must be taken into account.

Having said all of the above, don't be overly rigid with your schedule either. Something urgent to address in the business can and does happen (or there may be other unforeseen circumstances). Under these circumstances it's best to simply reschedule the meeting. Don't insist on having the meeting whatever happens when you know this will put both yourself and your employee in a stressful situation. This will not lead to a productive meeting in any case.

So, in summary, to make sure these meetings happen with optimal timing, the following should be considered:

- ➢ Meetings planned at least once a month
- ➢ Avoid meetings just after lunch
- ➢ Schedule meetings mid-morning or the middle of the afternoon where possible
- ➢ Avoid too early in the morning or too late in the evening

- ➢ Don't take people out of operations at peak times for meetings
- ➢ Where possible, schedule meetings on midweek days (Tuesday, Wednesday or Thursday)

If you follow the above as closely as possible (whilst taking into account your own operational constraints at the same time), you are likely to have meetings which are far more productive and you will have done everything possible to ensure that your employees are there not only in body but also in spirit.

Let's now go and have a look at just where we should be holding these meetings.

WHERE

One-to-One

Managing quality time with individuals for engagement and success

5WH

WHERE

Physical conditions and the immediate environment also need to be carefully considered when you plan your meetings. If, like many people you have a tendency to become drowsy when it's too hot in a room, you really must ensure that this is not the case during the one-to-one. As you can imagine, if both you and your employee start to fall asleep in the meeting it is not going to be optimal in terms of effectiveness. Of course, the opposite is also true: if the meeting is taking place where it's far too cold, you are probably going to have a very short meeting and not be able to concentrate even for a very short time.

A lot of recent research suggests that a real correlation exists between the temperature in an office and the level of productivity. The conclusion of this research is often that the optimal temperature for working is between 21°C and 23°C. Certain studies have shown that office workers made far fewer typing errors at these optimum temperatures and that up until 25°C, the incidence of errors decreased. Quite apart from anything else, being warm and comfortable is often associated with positive emotions such as a feeling of well-being and empathy.

As for the cold, from a physiological standpoint, your brain transfers energy to your body to keep you warm when exposed to conditions which are too cold, meaning that there is less energy available for concentration. Added to this, the cold is often associated with "feeling a bit low" or even "downright depression." So, even from a psychological point of view, holding a meeting in conditions which are too cold is not a good idea. This all might seem quite obvious, but I have been in meetings where the main subject of conversation at and during the meeting became the fact that "the heating's not working" or "the air conditioning is turned up too high." It is often the basic things that are forgotten when we are about to have an important discussion or meeting. Really, don't let this be the case for your one-to-one meetings.

What about other environmental parameters which we should pay attention to such as lighting or noise? Let's take lighting first. Bad lighting can have bad effects on health both on a physical and mental level. On the simplest level, bad levels of lighting can lead to eye strain, headaches and, in some cases, migraines which can of course be debilitating for some individuals. Psychologically, the lack of natural sunlight during the winter months leads to the disorder known as seasonal affective disorder (SAD). Certain studies suggest that during winter up to 40% of workers endure poor lighting conditions every day at work.

Several different studies carried out in Europe gave the following global results:

> ➤ Four in ten workers reported having uncomfortable lighting every day at work.
> ➤ One third said that better lighting would make them feel happier at work.

Added to this, medical research has shown that 13 to 15 minutes of exposure to natural light are enough to trigger the release of endorphins (or the happy hormones as they are commonly known).

From an entirely commonsense point of view, it would make sense to ensure that lighting is at the correct level where your meeting is taking place so that you can both actually see what you are doing! The studies and scientific evidence underline just how important it is to get this right. So, if you do have the opportunity, try to carry out your one-to-one in a space which has access to direct sunlight and (to state the obvious) do ensure that no one has the sunlight directly in their eyes!

Well, what about noise?

Obviously, if you are in a noisy environment this is not going to help at all. We have all heard the expression "there is so much noise that I can't hear myself think!"However, the level of noise does not have to be extremely loud; small incessant noise can do the same job on your concentration.

We all know that sources of noise such as those coming from telephones, air conditioning or traffic from a nearby road or construction site can be extremely irritating.

Other people's conversations can have a particularly adverse effect on optimal cognition (either on our own or that of our employee). For example, if we are holding our meeting next to a meeting room that does not have good soundproofing our concentration is very likely to become a "victim" of the "voices next door," and even more so, if there are large numbers of people in the meeting. Most often, this is due to what is known as the Lombard effect which describes the fact that people start talking more and more loudly as it gets louder around them.

A lot of research has been carried out which strongly suggests that the sound of other people's conversations is the noise which is the **most destructive** for our levels of concentration. In addition, there is further research showing that productivity can fall by as much as 20% in open-plan offices as a result. As a case in point, if you have been to a dinner where there are a large number of people, you probably have realised just how difficult it is to have an in-depth conversation with any one individual at the dinner. This is because, despite your best efforts not to, you will hear the conversations going on around you and you cannot "switch off the others" in order to attentively listen to the "one."

From what we've just seen, it's clearly very important indeed to choose the place of your meeting carefully in order to avoid noise interference which will reduce your levels of concentration. It is even more obvious that under no circumstances should you hold your meeting in an open-plan office with other co-workers present.

So, in summary, do ensure that the place you hold the meeting is:

- ➤ Correctly lit
- ➤ At the optimal temperature
- ➤ With the least interference from possible noise and, in particular, other people's conversations

Never forget the importance of ensuring the correct physical environment for your meeting. It would, after all, be such a shame to prepare all of the other aspects, only to have your meeting rendered completely ineffective by your physical surroundings. In addition, your collaborator will probably not take this well at all and may even see this as a lack of care or managerial competence on your part. At worst, he/she might think that you've done it on purpose.

Once you have ensured that the physical/environmental conditions where you are to hold the meeting are optimal, you can start to prepare on how to welcome your employee to his or her one-to-one.

In order to do this, you must ensure that you are prepared correctly, which means switching off your phone and ensuring that you won't be disturbed during the time allotted for the meeting. The only thing worse than your employee not being prepared for the meeting is that you've not prepared yourself! This will inevitably lead to the employee not taking the meeting seriously and you really don't want that to happen if you value using your time in an optimal manner. In addition, your employee might even lose respect for you and you don't want this to happen at any cost.

So, apart from ensuring that your assistant should be informed that you are not to be disturbed during the meeting and switching your phone off, what else do you need to prepare? Well, one thing is to make sure that you read the notes from the previous meeting beforehand so that you know what was said the last time, and what issues or subjects are supposed to be discussed during this meeting. Now we can go on to the welcoming phase.

In order to do this in the most optimal way possible, you have to know who is coming to the meeting well in advance. So, now that we have the right place for our meetings, just who exactly should be attending them?

WHO

One-to-One

Managing quality time with individuals for engagement and success

5WH

WHO

You should be having these meetings with every single person in your team. The qualifying condition is that the person should be reporting directly to you; in other words, you should be their immediate superior.

This point is extremely important and the task of meeting your direct reports is not something that can or should be delegated under any circumstances. The reasons for this are both extremely important and multiple. Try to imagine the impact of your own direct boss carrying out the one-to-one meetings with your subordinates. Some probable impacts of this would be as follows:

> ➢ It would cause a problem with your positioning as a leader for your subordinates (their perception of "yeah, he's the boss but not really")
> ➢ Your boss will not have the same level of knowledge about each of the employees as you do and this will degrade the quality of the meetings
> ➢ Your employees might be tempted to "go over your head" on a very frequent basis
> ➢ It will look like your boss does not trust you as a manager or leader

All of the above would of course lead to your total loss of credibility as a manager or leader and you would not have the opportunity to build relationships based on confidence and trust with your team members.

On the contrary, you should always ensure that it is you who carries out these meetings with your direct reports. It should also be underlined that you must carry out these meetings with every single direct report (barring none). You may have people in your team that you consider "more difficult" to manage than others and you might be tempted to spend as little time with them as possible. Well, the bad news is that it just does not work like that.

If there are "problems" with certain individuals in your teams, one-to-one meetings will perhaps give you a golden opportunity to "iron them out." Avoidance is not a good way to solve or resolve problems. On the contrary, avoidance tends to aggravate things and, in particular, in this case, if the person should realise that you are spending much less time with them than the others. However, a one-to-one is not the right place to conduct a disciplinary interview either. If this type of meeting is required, it should definitely be carried out separately from the regular one-to-one meeting.

Another extremely important aspect of "who," concerning quality time or one-to-one meetings, is who has ownership of these meetings? What I mean here is that we should remember that the meeting is the employee's meeting. So, although a meeting does require basic structure and formalisation, such as an agenda, and to be based on things such as defined goals and objectives, it is often a good idea to give some flexibility to the agenda in the sense that it should be the employee himself who prepares and sends the agenda. Or, at the very least, let the employee have a say on some of the content of the meeting.

This enables the employee to have some autonomy and be empowered to make decisions not only about which subjects are both important and urgent for discussion, but also to increase their sense of belonging to the "process" and to **take ownership of the process over time**. This also has a lot to do with engagement with both you as the boss and with the company or organisation in a more general way. Certain statistics show us that up to 85% of people in the workforce are either slightly disengaged or completely disengaged when asked about their feelings of belonging to the organisation. Some of the most important factors reported were boredom, lack of purpose and a lack of autonomy and empowerment.

Giving more ownership of the process to the employee would seem to be a good idea from this perspective and indeed it is. Do remember, though, that when you build relationships like this, people do not work for companies; they work for other people and, **in this case, that is you**. Do be careful then when "handing" ownership of this important process to the employee and ensure that he/she is ready to be empowered in this way. A good guide to when an employee is ready for this responsibility is that they are both extremely competent and motivated.

Although we have already stated that the "who" is all of the people who report to you, there is also the "who" that must be addressed on a grander scale, that of the organisation as a whole.

What I mean here is that it is not enough for these one-to-one meetings to take place at your level only. The one-to-one **culture** should be spread throughout the organisation or, as most people would tend to say, "cascaded down" throughout the organisation. What I'm talking about here is the importance of sharing the same beliefs throughout the organisation. For this reason, the one-to-one meeting is one of your most important management tools.

When people talk about culture and descriptions of it, you will often hear the phrase "the way things are done around here." If you are very senior in the organisation, it is in your interest to ensure that these meetings become the norm and are or become part of company culture. Just why is that? Well, to start with, if these meetings are not "cascaded" throughout the organisation, the transmission of information and communication becomes more difficult or, to put it another way, things become "lost in translation" because we are quite simply not using the same methods.

In addition, common sense would tell us that if we consider that this is the best and most effective method of managing individuals, why would we not ensure that this happens at all levels in the organisation? This is particularly crucial for middle managers who are just that (in the middle, I mean). If you don't already have a system of one-to-one meetings operating in the organisation, you certainly need to ensure that your middle management is thoroughly convinced of its necessity and adhere to it before cascading the idea throughout the company.

A great starting point would be to begin the process with the executive and middle management teams to ensure a coherent approach throughout the organisation.

Once done, we must ensure that everyone concerned is comfortable in carrying out these meetings. For this to happen, an agreed upon method on how to carry out these meetings is crucial. This is critical if we wish to give ourselves the maximum chance of successfully putting these meetings in place.

HOW

One-to-One

Managing quality time with individuals for engagement and success

5WH

HOW

If you are starting to put in place these meetings, the very first thing that you need to do is to inform the people with whom you are going to be having the meetings as to why you are going to start the meetings and when.

Once done, you can then start looking at exactly how you are going to make sure that these meetings are going to be as effective as possible. We have already seen some of the important elements which will help ensure that optimal conditions are created, such as planning the meetings at optimal times and ensuring that your employee has sufficient information about the meeting well in advance so that he or she can prepare for it. We have also already looked at the importance of the physical conditions of the space where the meeting will take place.

The welcoming phase of the one-to-one meeting is extremely important and, in particular, if your employee is not yet used to participating in this type of meeting. Just as when welcoming a friend to your home, you really do have to make sure that everything is done to prepare a great welcome and ensure that your team member feels completely at ease.

Therefore, when you welcome people to your office (or wherever you are carrying out the meeting), do ensure that you offer them something to drink, either a glass of water or a cup of coffee or tea. Do also ensure that there is always something to drink available during the meeting (at least water). Is it so important to offer something to drink? Well, I would say that it is as once again it shows care and attention to the employee in question and is the very least that we might do in terms of simple courtesy. Moreover, studies have shown that being even mildly dehydrated can affect your mental performance.

But what does it mean to be mildly dehydrated? It means that if you are around 2% dehydrated, you won't feel thirsty! Nevertheless, other similar studies have shown that even being **1% dehydrated** can cause **deficits** in your **visual and working memory.**

During the welcoming phase of the meeting, it is equally important to put your colleague at ease. To do this, make good eye contact, offer a firm handshake and ask them how they are. Then ask them "to make themselves comfortable" and offer them a seat. Once you're both seated, it's always a good thing to check if they are feeling comfortable (not too hot or cold, for example). Then it's always a good idea to start the meeting off with a short informal phase or some "small talk". You might want to get to the essence of the meeting and discuss what's on the agenda without further ado, but if you appear too rushed to do this your employee might not as yet be ready (or even willing in some cases).

For example, you might start the meeting by asking after your employee's family, what he/she did last weekend or has plans to do on the coming weekend? Remember that your employees are not always as used to having meetings as you are, so anything you can do to put them in a position where they feel comfortable talking to you is a real bonus.

Now it's time to get to the heart of the matter, that is to say, the formal part of the meeting. In order to "run" this part of the meeting in an optimal way there should be a certain amount of structure to it.

I find the following to be a good guide to structure this type of meeting:

SCOP

Sales

Costs

Operations

People

Let's take sales first. Under this heading, the employee does not have to work in sales; he could work in production or HR but that does not mean that he will not have ideas about how to improve the sales of your product or service. An "outside eye" can often be beneficial. For example, someone in production may have seen a way to modify the product itself and in so doing create a more saleable item. Another example might be the kitchen staff in a restaurant who notice that since the best-selling dish has been taken off the menu, there is a lot less activity in the restaurant (hence less sales). We could give countless examples here, but the point is that anyone in an organisation might have an idea about how to increase sales, so why ignore this possibility?

Of course, if the person is from sales, it gives the opportunity to discuss sales volumes and trends, possible improvements for the future and also what might be stopping sales potential from becoming optimal.

For the section concerning cost, you might want to discuss the cost of sales, the cost of production or the cost of personnel depending on which department in the organisation the employee belongs to. What I'm saying here is that there are always costs involved in the delivery of a service or product in any industrial activity or operation, and that to ensure maximum profitability, costs do have to be controlled and this is not only the responsibility of the Financial Controller or Director. It goes without saying though, that you might spend significantly more time on this area when speaking with an employee from finance to discuss areas such as cost of sales, cost ratios to revenue, trends in costs or rising costs of basic materials related to production.

Nevertheless, as with sales, it might just be that operations or customer-facing staff have some of the best ideas as far as cost efficiencies go.

Operations can also be discussed by nearly every employee in an organisation. The person does not have to be involved in operations in order to have a direct feeling or idea about how effective or efficient operations might be. Let's take the example of Human Resources (HR). If we imagine that a department cannot run effectively due to the constant lack of qualified staff, it could be that you will need to discuss with HR how you can go about recruiting the people necessary or finding a solution for the unusual level of turnover within the department.

People are a rather obvious subject that should be discussed in a one-to-one meeting, no matter where the employee comes from within the company or organisation. If we start with the employee who is participating in the one-to-one, we might be discussing his or her personal development, training needs, or relationships with colleagues. The employee's planning and his or her personal objectives for the year should also be discussed (this last one should be a fixed item in all one-to-one meetings). If you are having a one-to-one with someone at a management level, the themes will be the same but you will not be discussing only individual cases but also subjects coming from more of a team perspective.

Throughout all of these themes (SCOP), do ensure that smart objectives are attached to each of them to ensure a balanced scorecard approach. As discussed under "why" earlier, it is extremely important to ensure that you cover the SMART objectives agreed with the employee during the one-to-one. Once again, this will avoid unnecessary and unpleasant surprises during the end of the year review and it gives the employee the opportunity to ask for extra resources, help or indeed more time, if and when necessary.

You are of course completely free to use another framework to run your one-to-one meetings. The advantage of the SCOP is that it is a tried and tested method so why take time to reinvent the wheel?

Now that we've talked about giving structure to your meetings, let's discuss some of the behavioural aspects that are important to the effectiveness of this type of meeting.

Let's talk first about interruptions to the purpose or, more accurately, the structure of the meeting. Let us imagine that you are halfway into the meeting and the employee suddenly wants to discuss a personal issue which is obviously very important to him or her. Even if this does interfere with the work-related discussion, you really do have time to listen to your employee in this type of situation even if you don't manage to achieve the objectives which you originally set for this meeting. **This is extremely important**. Do remember that one of the reasons that you are holding these meetings is to instil confidence and trust both with individuals and within your team. If you decide to tell the employee that you can't listen to them because it's not directly work related, you will be making a big mistake! This once again underlines the importance of the Theodore Roosevelt quote mentioned earlier:

"People don't care how much you know until they know how much you care." I will not apologise for repeating this quote because it is fundamentally important to this book and the whole belief system (or culture) surrounding the one-to-one.

Furthermore, I would argue that problems of this kind are work related, in the sense that when people have problems outside of work, it often interferes in a negative way with their performance and productivity at work. This can be the case with people at all levels in the organisation including high performers. Secondly, if you are serious about creating a work environment in which people are happy and have both confidence and trust in their management and leaders, you have no choice but to listen. This does not mean that you will have a solution to whatever the problem is but you will have demonstrated empathy and a caring attitude. You may even be able to indicate where the person might be able to find professional help in certain cases and depending on the situation at hand. The mere fact of taking the time to really listen can already be of great help and benefit both to yourself and your employee. Of course, this does not have to be a problem from outside work; it can also be more directly related to a situation at work. Imagine that you have not taken the time to listen to problems regarding things such as bullying, moral or sexual harassment, or problems related to violence of any nature, whether verbal or physical.

In ignoring or not giving due consideration or credence to these types of situations, you are putting your employee, yourself, and the organisation as a whole at risk!

This brings us neatly to our second point regarding behaviours to adopt – that of listening itself. Pareto's rule would indicate that in this type of meeting we should be listening as a manager 80% of the time and only talking during 20%. As a general principle, this is a good guideline, but one not stuck to by managers stringently enough. As an example, I once went to a senior colleague of mine to ask his advice about how I was managing my individual team members and his response – which was "we are all prisoners of what we say but masters of our own silence" – certainly gave me food for thought! As a young manager, I was always thinking about what I was going to say next instead of actually listening to what was being said. As Jimmy Hendrix once said:

"Knowledge speaks, but wisdom listens."

So, do remember that you are not holding a one-to-one meeting to display the in-depth level of your knowledge in order to "impress the hell out of your employee." **You are there first and foremost to listen to him or her.**

When thinking about how to carry out one-to-one meetings, the earlier Roosevelt quote is just so important! Especially when you consider that the act of attentively listening to your team member will, apart from anything else, act as the glue which will go toward reinforcing your working relationship with them.

Nevertheless, as always, there can be exceptions to this 80/20 rule such as when a junior employee is having his or her first one-to-one with their manager and they're not yet confident enough to talk openly or in enough detail. Your job here will be to find ways in which to encourage the employee to talk by listening attentively to what he or she does say and then asking pertinent questions regarding what was just said or by asking for more details or explanations.

Then, when they do start to express themselves more easily and with confidence, you must ensure that you are listening very attentively indeed. One of the most common habits that people have when they are "listening" to someone is a tendency to be thinking about how they are going to answer the question or about what they want to say in reply instead of actually hearing and understanding what is being said to them. I'm sure that we have all done this at one time or another; I know that I have and it has caused me some very awkward and embarrassing moments in the past!

If, added to this, you are in a noisy environment, as spoken about earlier; it's easy to see the almost infinite number of possibilities either for a complete lack of understanding during the meeting and/or misunderstandings occurring following the meeting. So, this leads us all to the following question: can we learn to be a good or at least a better listener? The good news here is that there are some tried and tested techniques that can be learned and which have proven to be extremely effective in this regard.

For me, one of the most important secrets of good listening is what I like to call attentive listening. This helps to train oneself to break the previously mentioned habit of planning one's reply and instead listen very attentively to what the other says.

There are several important stages involved in being or becoming a better listener during one-to-one conversations. First, being attentive during the conversation means giving 100% of your attention to the person who's in front of you and not, for example, sending or answering an SMS when you are meant to be listening to them. It also involves, as we said earlier, not formulating your answers or your own questions mentally whilst you are supposed to be listening and training yourself to do this in an active manner. It certainly doesn't involve leaving the meeting to answer a telephone call under any circumstances!

Asking open questions is very important if you wish to have a fulfilling conversation. If you constantly ask questions such as "Do you agree with that?" or "Is that a good or a bad thing?" you will constantly get yes or no answers, which can quickly make a conversation very short or make it seem very long (not to mention a bit one-sided). In place of those questions, you could ask, for example, "Why exactly do you disagree with that?" or "What makes you say that what we've just said is a good or a bad thing?" You will receive more information and, not only that; you will constantly be encouraging the person you're with to express their opinion.

Probing questions exist to give detail and context whilst, at the same time, showing real interest in the answer that you have just been given to the open question. So, questions such as "Could you give me some more detail?" or "More specifically, what did you mean in your last point?" can help to get useful detail and give more context to your discussion.

Requesting clarification is just that; use a phrase or question such as "I'm sorry, but I'm not quite sure that I understood. Could you explain to me again, I didn't understand some of the jargon used?" This can be particularly useful when speaking to someone who has very specific expertise and is used to speaking with his colleagues in their "own language." Common examples might be IT people, engineers or finance people trying to explain things "in laymen's terms" to others. Also, remember that a lot of the time those that you are having the conversation with will have a lot more expertise in their own field than you do so that this can prove to be a very helpful technique.

Another technique that's sometimes useful in dealing with experts is what I like to call "the 3 Whys" technique. Basically, by the time that you have asked why three times about the expert's original answer to a question you should get to the level of detail or simplification needed for you to understand.

When you have clarification and think that you have understood perfectly, paraphrasing is an extremely good way to make sure that you have. For example, you might say something like "So, if I understood correctly, this means that you have found a way to improve the quality of production, is that right?" In this way, you are doing two things. First, you are showing that you have been listening and are interested in what has been said. Secondly, you are checking that you have perfectly understood and are giving an opportunity to the other person to correct or give further detail or context.

It's also important to pay attention to how the person is feeling during the meeting and to try and reflect those feelings. Paying attention to feelings may seem obvious, but does mean paying attention to both verbal and non-verbal communication. For example, if your employee is talking about an enormous problem, for example, a huge problem communicating with one of his or her subordinates or superiors and seems to be quite emotional regarding this subject, one of the worst things to do might be to brush it off and show the employee a big "toothy grin" whilst telling them that they're making too much of it!

It would be better to perhaps listen to the employee in this type of situation and ask them how you might help them resolve this issue. Better yet, ask them if they themselves already have the beginnings of a solution.

With regards to non-verbal communication, an example might be that when the employee is listening to you, he or she leans forward and shows that they are listening attentively. Imagine now that during the one-to-one with the same employee, you constantly sit back in an extremely relaxed position every time that they are talking (and leaning toward you). From his or her point of view, do you think they'll have the impression that you are listening attentively, if at all?

To show and demonstrate empathy during a one-to-one conversation is important. A lot has been written about the fact that mirroring the attitudes, postures and behaviours of someone during a meeting can be highly effective in increasing the efficiency of the communication process and creating empathy and trust.

The types of techniques and behavioural analysis just mentioned are the backbone of what has come to be known as Neuro-Linguistic Programming (NLP).

At the end of your conversation, it's important to summarise, which is not the same thing as paraphrasing. The important thing here is to cover the main points or to highlight the most important points made during the discussion and to gain agreement as to how to move forward from there (in the next meeting or by agreeing on definite objectives or actions within a given time frame).

We must also ensure at this stage that adequate written notes have been taken by the employee so that he or she will be in a position to send you a written summary of what was talked about and agreed upon during the meeting well before the next one. This will once again introduce a structured approach to your meetings and avoid wasting time by going over "old ground."

Something not yet mentioned is the veritable power of silence! Try not to slip into the all too familiar habit of answering your own questions either partially or fully. Remember what we spoke about earlier, the fact that we should always be asking open questions. What was not mentioned is that **we have to give people time to respond to these questions.** Do remember that not everyone is as used to being in meetings as you are and that people are very different in the way that they react to questions. Sometimes a long silence only means that the person you are talking to is giving due consideration to what you've just said and is thinking about it. So don't make the mistake of asking another question too quickly.

Furthermore, do try and take into account people's preferences or preferred methods or modes of communication. This really does help ensure the success of your one-to-one meetings. Normally this should be self-evident but not always!

As an example, you may well spend the majority of time speaking to your financial director about finance and subjects related to finance; this does not mean that you always have to take a highly analytical approach to every finance question. As someone's manager, you might and should have access to their psychological profile or the psychometric tests completed by the person upon entry to the organisation when they joined (or after). For example, these types of test can give you information about critical thinking skills, likely reactions to stressful situations or information regarding preferred behaviours or patterns of behaviour. Commonly, we might want to measure to what point someone has a preference for creativity, analysis, organisation or a more empathetic mode of functioning.

If you do have this information, you should be using it to good effect and of course with the best of intentions. For me, there are however two very important distinctions to be made about these types of tests. First, they are carried out at one point in time and people do evolve over time and, secondly and more importantly, they tend to give us an idea of **preference only!**

What I mean here is that these tests do not define who people are; they merely give some indications regarding preferred behaviours or "ways to function." Taking an example here, we might be sure that the preferred way of "functioning" of our finance director has nothing to do with what we might have first assumed. Imagine that we had thought of him or her as someone who always wanted to analyse everything and was only focused on details and was never really interested in doing anything which might be considered in any way creative including, of course, creative accounting (excuse the pun). What if we are mistaken and that he or she is an extremely creative individual who has tremendous ideas for developing our business in ways that we have never even considered or thought about?

Just imagine that we have never asked them if they have any ideas on how we might change or improve things? Once again, we must give people the opportunity to express their thoughts, feelings, opinions and ideas.

Do not assume that someone will act or react in the way which you might expect given their job role. Do remember that if you assume too much, you are likely to be very wide of the mark indeed. Remember the old adage "Assume makes an ASS out of U and Me." More importantly, if you do make assumptions about someone without taking the time to get to know them properly, this can and will be taken for a lack of respect.

Using appropriate listening skills and techniques together with a good understanding of your people will allow you to form relationships which will not only be valuable, but also long lasting. This, in turn, will ensure the fluidity and effectiveness of two way communication during your meetings.

This may seem like a fairly time-consuming process at the beginning, but with time and practice, you will find that acquiring these skills will help you run more effective meetings.

Last, but not least, the one-to-one is the best place to give constructive feedback to your employee. We all know how easy this is if the feedback to be given is positive. It's not difficult to congratulate someone for doing a tremendous job after all. The one qualifying condition for giving positive feedback is however that it is well deserved and well explained. After all, if you are constantly telling someone what a brilliant job they are doing, but this is not based on verifiable facts, it will soon become entirely meaningless.

On the other hand, do not fall into the trap of never congratulating at all and only giving constant feedback on areas for improvement. Even small wins can be extremely important for employees. Don't forget to celebrate success as this is key to both employee motivation and engagement. Having said all of this, feedback is not always of a positive nature, unfortunately. Sometimes, you will need to give feedback about the required improvements concerning the performance or behaviour of certain team members.

This is something that must not be avoided at any cost. Often, younger or less experienced managers have a tendency to "smooth over" or "brush aside" matters of concern so as to "keep the peace" so to speak. This is a terrible mistake and can lead to more serious issues with the concerned individual as well as with the team. After all, as a manager, you must be seen to be fair to all members of the team from both an individual and collective point of view.

Still, it's not always pleasant or easy to give "negative feedback" to a team member. Fortunately, there is a very good management technique which can help us with this.

I call this the **EASY** method:

Explain to the team member the exact nature of the problem, area for improvement, unacceptable behaviour or lower than normal performance. Also explain what the consequences or effects of this behaviour or problem have been. As an example, you might have to explain how the behaviour in question has negatively affected the financial results of the department for which they work or perhaps even the company as a whole. Another example, could be explaining how the problem might have affected other team members.

Ask him or her if they have understood exactly what you have said to them and check thoroughly for understanding. The second part of ask involves you asking them if they have a solution for what has happened or if they know how to prevent a recurrence in the future. This is extremely important and you should spend time here. This allows for a participative approach which involves the team member finding or helping find a solution. The objective here is to give your employee purpose and to avoid placing blame. Your role during this stage of the process will be that of a coach helping your team member reach conclusions and/or find prospective solutions.

Solve Yourself. In certain cases, the employee may not find the appropriate answer or solution to the problem. In these cases you are going to have to be more directive and point out the required solution to the problem. In this instance, your role will be more that of a mentor rather than a coach in explaining exactly what the solution is going to be and ensuring that it is understood.

Whether the situation is solved in a participative or a more direct manner, agreement still has to be reached as to how the corrective action is to be put in place. Once this is understood, and as a last step, the consequences of either success or failure putting in place the corrective action(s) must be made clear to him or her.

This method may at first seem quite simple but, like a lot of other things in management, it requires a lot of practice in order for it to become second nature.

When giving this type of feedback, you should also ensure that your tone of voice and body language are giving the same message as the words that you are using (i.e., you should not be smiling or laughing when giving this type of feedback). In other words, there should not be a dichotomy between your verbal and non-verbal language. If this happens, at the very least the communication will be ineffective or misunderstood and at worst will lead to unnecessary conflict.

Do, however, remember that there is a big difference between giving constructive feedback on a difficult point or area for improvement to someone and a disciplinary interview. The regular one-to-one meeting is not the place for discipline or disciplinary procedures. If this is required at any stage, this must be the object of an entirely different meeting.

For me, there are four important words to bear in mind constantly when you are giving feedback to one of your team:

Be   **Honest**

Be   **Fair**

Be   **Direct**

Be   **Consistent**

If you stick to this when you are giving feedback (whether negative or positive), you won't go far wrong and, indeed, in this way, you will gain the respect of the individuals who make up your team.

CONCLUSION

One-to-One

Managing quality time with individuals for engagement and success

5WH

CONCLUSION

As in many other areas of business and management, there are a number of variables which are important and which need to be taken into account if we wish to succeed. For most businesses they would be considered to be things such as:

- ➤ Economic adaptability
- ➤ Pricing and pricing strategies
- ➤ Best use of available resources (human, capital, financial or intangible)
- ➤ Quality (of service, best in class product, process, etc.)

These common denominating factors can, of course, vary in terms of their comparative importance depending on the sector of activity or industry that you find yourself in. For a given sector or industry, these are called the key success factors, basically meaning that if any of them are missing it is going to become increasingly difficult to ensure or indeed sustain a high level of performance.

In the practice of management, there are a lot of things that are known to be best practice or key success factors as just defined. Throughout the preceding pages, what I have attempted to do is to underline a number of areas which are key success factors for optimising the efficiency and effectiveness of one-to-one meetings with your employees and team members.

As a summary, and in order to reunite all of the key success factors for holding one-to-one meetings (or quality time), I have produced the following diagram as a summary and reminder:

The key success factors then are:

- ➢ Meetings should be **prepared in advance** so that all parties are correctly prepared for the meeting and advised of the content of the meeting in advance (such as the agenda). Remember the five P's of planning here: **Proper Planning Prevents Poor Performance**.
- ➢ **Meetings are planned regularly** to ensure that relationships are correctly formed over time and that they are planned at **times which are convenient** as well as **possible** for both participants.
- ➢ The optimal **environmental and physical conditions** must be in place during the meeting to ensure that you and the participant are "100% in the meeting" and not distracted either by physical discomfort or intrusions on your concentration such as other people's conversations nearby.
- ➢ A **warm welcome should be extended to the participant** at the beginning of the meeting to ensure his or her comfort within the meeting environment and to ensure that he/she is at ease and has the opportunity to **communicate in an optimum way**.
- ➢ Give **structure** to the meeting to **facilitate** both the recurrent nature of the meeting and to ensure the efficiency of **follow up** on any outstanding issues and the participant's

main objectives. This also allows the meeting to "flow" smoothly.

➤ Use your **attentive listening skills** during the meeting to enhance **communication** and further **build confidence and trust** with your employee.

➤ Remember that the participant owns the meeting. This does not mean that he or she "runs" the meeting. What it does mean is:

  o He/she should be doing most of the talking.

  o He/she should take the notes from the meeting on a document to be sent to you before the next meeting.

  o He/she should be offering content for the meeting and for the agenda.

  o We are talking mainly about the participant's objectives, goals, development, ideas and operational concerns during the meeting.

These key success factors will allow you to have both productive and efficient meetings. They will also allow you to enhance the quality of the content of the meeting and build quality relationships with your subordinates.

Something else, which is of the utmost importance, is having a commonly shared frame of reference with your team member as to how tasks should be prioritised.

A great way to do this is to use what I like to call the 3 P method concerning tasks for completion:

- ➢ Prioritise
- ➢ Plan
- ➢ Promote

Prioritise

Tasks here are not only important but that need to be completed either the same day or in the very near future. In the context of one-to-one meetings, it's extremely important that there is a shared understanding as to what qualifies as a priority.

Plan

Is a task which is still important, but does not have to be carried out in the immediate future; it does, however, as the name indicates, need to be planned. Typically, you will find action plans here with specific due dates which should of course in the majority of cases bear some relation to the goals and objectives of the team member in question.

Promote

These are tasks which are not yet priorities and are not yet planned. They are therefore tasks which can be "promoted" to either a priority or that can be planned (or not).

There should be a shared belief in the importance of planning and preparation and how dynamic it needs to be; remember the saying:

"If you fail to plan, you are planning to fail."

Finally, if there is one thing that all managers and leaders need to remember, it is that the creation of value for your customers is inherently based on the value created first and foremost by your employees. So, not spending adequate time nurturing the individuals who make up this invaluable resource is never (past, present or future) a good choice, whether voluntary or otherwise.

These one-to-one meetings are an integral part of the creation of internal value for your internal customers (your employees) together with other areas such as training, recognition programs, proper recruitment and selection, good working conditions and overall care of and attention to the individuals who make up your workforce.

These meetings are also one of the strongest and most important links to the service profit chain. To recap, this chain is based on the idea that there is a very high correlation between providing great service to your employees and higher staff retention (leading to lower recruitment, induction and training costs). It also, of course, means better engagement and loyalty, leading in turn to higher and better levels of production (better quality and productivity). All of this eventually leads to an increase in customer satisfaction, brand loyalty and sales.

Ultimately, this leads to a situation which is more profitable for all concerned; yourself, your employee and your organisation.

To put all of this "in a nutshell:"

Never forget that it is your employees who create the value which is consumed by your customers.

At the beginning of this book we saw the various negative and indeed disastrous effects of not taking employee engagement seriously enough. Page after page, use has been made of empirical evidence, scientific studies, as well as management techniques and knowledge which have consistently pointed towards the critical importance of engagement.

Throughout the book, one of the most dominant ideas or paradigms is that of the individual employee as the internal customer and the primary resource. An awful lot has been written about customer relationship management (or CRM) but today a new "chapter" needs to be written about employee relationship management (ERM).

In the years to come, ERM will become more and more fundamental to strategies which aim to sustain competitive advantage for all companies and organisations. At the very core of these strategies we are going to find that running effective one-to-one meetings will no longer be optional.